RISE
AND
REJOICE

HEATHER
MURDOCK

RISE
AND
REJOICE

A HEART TRANSFORMATION
JOURNEY FOR WOMEN

© 2022 by Heather Murdock. All rights reserved.

Published by Redemption Press, PO Box 427, Enumclaw, WA 98022.
Toll-Free (844) 2REDEEM (273-3336)

Redemption Press is honored to present this title in partnership with the author. The views expressed or implied in this work are those of the author. Redemption Press provides our imprint seal representing design excellence, creative content, and high-quality production.

The author has tried to recreate events, locales, and conversations from memories of them. In order to maintain their anonymity, in some instances the names of individuals, some identifying characteristics, and some details may have been changed, such as physical properties, occupations, and places of residence.

Noncommercial interests may reproduce portions of this book without the express written permission of the author, provided the text does not exceed five hundred words. When reproducing text from this book, include the following credit line: "*Rise and Rejoice* by Heather Murdock. Used by permission."

Commercial interests: No part of this publication may be reproduced in any form, stored in a retrieval system, or transmitted in any form by any means—electronic, photocopy, recording, or otherwise—without prior written permission of the publisher/author, except as provided by United States of America copyright law.

Unless otherwise indicated, all Scripture quotations are from the Holy Bible, New International Version®, NIV®. Copyright © 1973, 1978, 1984, 2011 by Biblica, Inc.™ Used by permission of Zondervan. All rights reserved worldwide. www.zondervan.com The "NIV" and "New International Version" are trademarks registered in the United States Patent and Trademark Office by Biblica, Inc.™

Scripture quotations marked (MSG) are taken from THE MESSAGE, copyright © 1993, 2002, 2018 by Eugene H. Peterson. Used by permission of NavPress, represented by Tyndale House Publishers. All rights reserved.

Scripture quotations marked (NLT) are taken from the Holy Bible, New Living Translation, copyright ©1996, 2004, 2015 by Tyndale House Foundation. Used by permission of Tyndale House Publishers, Carol Stream, Illinois 60188. All rights reserved.

Scripture quotations marked (TPT) are taken from The Passion Translation®. Copyright © 2017, 2018 by Passion & Fire Ministries, Inc. Used by permission. All rights reserved. ThePassionTranslation.com.

Scripture quotations marked (KJV) are taken from the New King James Version®. Copyright © 1982 by Thomas Nelson. Used by permission. All rights reserved.

ISBN 13: 978-1-64645-570-6 (Paperback)
978-1-64645-569-0 (ePub)
978-1-64645-568-3 (Mobi)

Library of Congress Catalog Card Number: 2021923772

Contents

Introduction 9
Week 1: Do you want to be free? 13
Week 2: "Who Do You Say I Am?" 23
Week 3: "Do You Understand What I've Done for You?" . . . 31
Week 4: "Are You Listening to Me?" 39
Week 5: "Do You Really Love Me?" 49
Week 6: "Do You Believe Me?" 59
As You Rise 69

Introduction

Dear sister,

Welcome to the *Rise and Rejoice* heart transformation study. You are invited to a divine feast.

A banquet of abundance.

A table overflowing with sumptuous food and drink that will restore, refresh, and revive your heart and soul.

When you dine at this table, you will be fully satisfied. You will not leave hungry, and your heart will be full and free. You will enjoy the intimate fellowship and connection you have longed for—that you were made for. You will rise and rejoice, and your heart will sing forever the praises of the One who not only invited you to His table, but prepared a place for you.

I'm both honored and delighted that you have decided to join me on this journey of inner heart healing. In this study, you will learn to trust the Lord with your deepest need, to open your heart to Him so that you may experience the freedom, joy, and peace He promises throughout His Word. Isaiah 55 tells us that in Jesus we are fully satisfied, yet we still look to other people, places, and things to satisfy us and tell us who we are. Every one of us has an identity God created that is found in an intimate relationship with Him. But we often look for our identity and value in people and their opinions of us. We search for our worth in money, success, reputation, status, career, and titles, just to name a few. This is because of the condition of our heart. Unresolved pain and unforgiveness affect our thoughts, feelings, and actions. The Bible teaches us that everything in our lives is impacted by the condition of our heart: "Above all else, guard your heart, for everything you do flows from it" (Proverbs 4:23).

In this study, we will ask the Holy Spirit to examine our hearts with His loving care and tenderness. We will ask Him into the deepest places where we've built barriers and waged wars. In our attempt to protect ourselves, we've put up walls where nothing can come in and nothing can get out. Our hearts have become hardened in this process. Slowly they have become immovable, defensive, and brittle. We hold on to wounds and unforgiveness like a warm blanket, as they become our security and identity. We have difficulty trusting people. We play it safe. We hide in the shadows of the past instead of resting in the shade of God's mercy.

That is not the life the Lord has planned for us. When we allow Jesus into our depths, our hidden holes, our secret sins, we allow the fullness of who He is to fill the hollow of who we are. We experience healing and wholeness. God has a plan of redemption and restoration for all of us. He promises a new heart—a heart full of His Spirit. A heart that's open, resilient, and hopeful. "And I will give you a new heart, and I will put a new spirit in you. I will take out your stony, stubborn heart and give you a tender, responsive heart" (Ezekiel 36:26 NLT).

I invite you to go deeper. To taste freedom. Sweet freedom. You will notice in the study there are sections called "Dig Deeper," which contain discipleship questions in weeks 2-6. As you go through those sections, let Jesus ask you the questions and practice talking to Him as you answer.

You will also notice sections called "Prayer Prompt," which offer specific prayers to help align your heart with the Lord and empower you to apply what you are learning.

My hope and prayer for you is that you experience the healing and freedom you have longed for. I pray you will not only discover your purpose, but that you will believe you are known, chosen, and

INTRODUCTION

called by God. I long for you to experience a life of intimate love, joy, and peace as you walk with Jesus. I encourage you to share this book with other women who are bound by pain and the lie that they are damaged beyond repair. I pray the grace and truth of Jesus will heal and transform your heart as you learn to trust Him with your greatest needs. I believe you will experience healing and freedom as you discover how the Lord wants to transform your pain into purpose. I pray you discover intimacy with Jesus is your greatest treasure and that you make spending time with Him in the secret place of your soul the priority of your life.

I've woven my testimony into this study so that you can understand who I am and where my heart is in leading women into a more intimate relationship with Jesus. He has worked miracles in my life, and I'm honored to share them with you.

WEEK 1

Do you want to be free?

John 8:36

SEVERAL YEARS AGO, I SAW A PRAYER COUNSELOR FOR SOME fears I was experiencing. She challenged me to daily sit with Jesus and ask Him to tell me what I don't know that I don't know that I don't know. Let that sink in.

At first, nothing happened.

For several days, I sat awkwardly in my alone time with Jesus waiting for some sort of new breakthrough. Nothing. Then one morning after a few weeks, I drove to work and heard the Holy Spirit say, "You've never been intimate with anyone. Not even your husband." I pulled off the road, stunned. I argued with God. "That's not true! That's so not true! Of course I have. How could you say that?"

What came next was a wave of revelation that left me in a puddle of tears. Of course it was true. Oh my wretched soul! I had overcome so much brokenness in my life through God's grace and forgiveness; how could I still be so messed up? I felt anguish, guilt, shame, and discouragement. But I also felt something else the next day when I confessed it to my dear friend: hope. I felt renewed hope that Jesus was going to help me get to the root of my fear of emotional intimacy. You see, I had been asking the Lord into deep places of hurt I had protected for years. I knew I needed deeper healing, but I didn't know the root of my pain. I was struggling with fears I wasn't willing to let control me any longer.

This revelation from the Holy Spirit filled me with courage and anticipation. I know the Lord reveals what He plans to heal. This started a journey of discovery I will share parts of throughout this study. On one of my mornings with Jesus, I was journaling, and led by the Spirit, I wrote this sentence: *Your greatest need becomes your greatest opportunity to experience the greatness of God's love and power.*

I've been meditating on this truth for several years. What I've learned is when we allow Jesus full access to our heart—and get really honest about our deepest need, our secret sin, the shame infected parts of our soul—we experience His love like a flood of forgiveness, like a rushing river, like a saving salve on the wounds of our heart and soul.

We find His grace runs deeper than our scars.

We rarely allow Jesus into these deep, dark places. We only allow Him into the shallow, safe spaces—the places where we have control. But it's for total freedom that we have been set free by Jesus.

Our hurts are an invitation to more of Jesus, which means more love, hope, faith, power, healing, depth, and purpose. It means more joy, more peace. More goodness. More freedom. Theologically and positionally, we are a new creation when we accept Jesus as our Savior. "Therefore, if anyone is in Christ, the new creation has come: The old has gone, the new is here!" (2 Corinthians 5:17).

John 8:36 (NIV) tells us we are free and "who the Son sets free is free indeed." The word "indeed" means truly, undeniably, and without question. What a promise! At the moment of salvation, the Holy Spirit begins transforming us more and more into the likeness of Jesus. This is a lifelong process and one that won't be completed to perfection until we are with Jesus in heaven. We can count on this promise from Philippians 1:6: "He who began a good work in us will carry it on to completion until the day of Christ Jesus."

He is faithful to complete the good work He has started. It's in this sanctifying process of being made holy that we learn to walk out our freedom and our new identity. We learn to walk out in the natural what has already been accomplished in the spiritual. The Holy Spirit invites us to a deeper level of love, trust, and oneness with God. With deeper trust comes more freedom as we learn to listen and to obey what He is leading us to do. Obedience is a key to freedom. When we hold onto our old identity and old coping mechanisms, we stay stuck. It's the letting go and letting God have lordship of our lives that gives us ultimate freedom.

I'm reminded of the monkey who wanted the banana in the jar. When he grabbed a hold of the banana, he couldn't get his hand out without letting go of it. He remained stuck as long as he held onto the banana. We don't realize that the things we think we want are also the things keeping us stuck.

When the Holy Spirit opens our hearts and minds to reveal our greatest need, He shines the healing light of His love into the darkness of our pain to deliver and restore us. His role is to make us more and more Christlike. His desire is that we will join Him on mission to make Jesus known to the world. He promises He will restore the years the locusts have eaten (Joel 2:25).

Let's begin this healing journey by identifying your greatest need and how it has shaped your life.

What is your greatest fear?

_____
_____
_____
_____
_____
_____
_____
_____
_____
_____

What is your greatest need? We often find our greatest need is to feel loved, or to feel worthy. Or maybe it's that we want to feel secure, accepted, or significant. Whatever it is for you, write it here and give yourself time to think it through. Ask the Holy Spirit to help you identify it.

___

Now let's see how your greatest need has been shaping your decisions and choices. What have you been doing to meet your need?

___

What have you been doing to stifle your need?

___

DO YOU WANT TO BE FREE?

What lies have you believed?

_____
_____
_____
_____
_____
_____
_____
_____

What traps have you stumbled into?

_____
_____
_____
_____
_____
_____
_____
_____

What price have you paid?

_____
_____
_____
_____
_____
_____
_____
_____

Jesus paid the ultimate price on the cross to set you free. He died to save you from your sins. You don't have to pay the price any longer. What is the Holy Spirit saying to you right now?

___

What are your thoughts?

___

What do you think Jesus is thinking about what you are thinking?

___

Your greatest need becomes your greatest opportunity to experience the greatness of God's love and power.

Proverbs 4:23 tells us, "Above all else, guard your heart, for everything you do flows from it." What's the condition of your heart? Write about where your heart is right now. Later, we will take a closer look with the help of an assessment tool.

_____
_____
_____
_____
_____
_____
_____
_____
_____

The answer to that question has a profound effect on the quality of your relationships and the quality of your entire life. The condition of your heart impacts how you show up as wife, mom, daughter, friend, leader, sister, grandmother, follower of Jesus, and every other role.

Are you angry, lonely, tired, bitter, sad, jealous? Are you nursing grudges, or nurturing grace? For yourself? For others? Where is this true in your life?

_____
_____
_____
_____
_____
_____
_____
_____

Dig Deeper

Much of my past is very painful. When I became a new believer, the Lord began miraculous works of healing. His presence in my life filled me with a wondrous kind of joy, peace, and love that I'd never known. He blessed me with favor and kindness. It was almost like He was wooing me. I still feel the Lord is making up for all those years. I remember reading Joel 2:25 and thinking, *Wow, I'm walking in that promise right now.*

The years the locusts have eaten are the years wrapped in regret. They are the lost years. What are the years the locusts have eaten in your life?

_____
_____
_____
_____
_____
_____
_____
_____
_____
_____

No one can turn back the hands of time, yet here God promises the impossible; an abundant harvest will follow the years of dry desolation. But this requires us to say yes to God. To let Him into our greatest need. He already knows what it is. He's not ashamed of you. He's not shocked by you. He's calling you by name. Right where you are, right now. Write about it.

_____
_____
_____
_____
_____
_____
_____

Prayer Prompt

I'm so proud of you! I've asked you to jump in the deep end the first week. This is difficult work, but it is good work. Heart work. I'm praying each of you will allow the Holy Spirit to minister to your heart as He continues to reveal your greatest need. Remember, He reveals what He will heal. Pray the promise of Joel 2:25: "I will restore the years the locusts have eaten." This promise is fulfilled when we say yes to God.

Jesus, you are my Healer and Redeemer. Thank You for the gentle and humble way You work within me. I believe You will restore to me what has been lost in Your perfect way and timing. Help me trust the process and surrender to Your Spirit working in me. Father, help me identify my greatest need and let You fulfill it. Help me open myself to You and teach me how to live in Your presence.

WEEK 2

"Who Do You Say I Am?"

Mark 8:29

DECEMBER 18, 1994, IS A DAY I WILL NEVER FORGET. A DAY marked by such horrific pain, I doubted I would ever escape its onslaught. Soul suffocation. My heart hammered into a million pieces. I dropped the phone and sunk to the floor, as darkness closed in around me like the blackest night. I remember little about the following hours except my dear friend, Sheila, picked me up and didn't let go until I ended up in the seat of an airplane for a flight home. A drunk driver had killed my sister. She and three friends had been driving home from The Nutcracker ballet in Sacramento, when a man on his way home from his company Christmas party hit them head on. I couldn't breathe. I wanted to die. Why couldn't it have been me?

That dark day collided with a wounded girl running from her past. That girl was me. A past scarred by shame. I had run all the way to the other side of the country, running to outdistance the confusion and hurt from my childhood. I was a girl with stars in my eyes, hoping to find myself in the glittering lights of fame and fortune in Hollywood and New York.

Ironically, before the accident I wanted to go home, back to Northern California where I grew up, but didn't know how. I was afraid of going home and admitting I failed, that I didn't make it in the Big City, the city that promised you everything and left you with nothing.

Willow's death brought me home.

The road to redemption was long and winding and full of detours. For many years after her death, I made choices that hurt me and others. I grieved in self-sabotage, secretly blaming myself, God, and ultimately Don, the man who gave the car keys to Kyle, the drunk driver. If only I'd been there, if only God had intervened, if only Kyle hadn't been so careless. If only Don hadn't been so stupid. If only . . .

> My eyes grow weak with sorrow, my soul and body with grief. My life is consumed by anguish and my years by groaning; my strength fails because of my affliction, and my bones grow weak. (Psalm 31:9–10)

At seventeen—six years before the accident—I entered a local beauty pageant, and a friend confided how she'd been throwing up to lose weight. I never had a weight problem, but I would be walking on stage in a bathing suit. What could it hurt to drop a few pounds? What started as an experiment became a twenty-year addiction, an addiction that caused self-loathing, deceit, and more shame.

Read all of Isaiah 55 (NKJV) before going further.

Here we see Jesus is everything our hearts desire. We can find everything we seek in Him. He has prepared a banquet of abundance for us. In Him we have no lack and are fully satisfied. So why do we go to other things, people, and places for fulfillment? The answer can be found in the condition of our hearts.

Invitation to the thirsty:

> Ho! Everyone who thirsts, come to the waters; and you who have no money, come, buy and eat. Yes, come, buy wine and milk without money and without price. Why do you spend money for what is not bread, and your wages for what does not satisfy? Listen carefully to me,

and eat what is good, and let your soul delight itself in abundance. (Isaiah 55:1–2)

What are you hearing in these first two verses?

_____

_____

_____

_____

The word "ho" means an important announcement. The prophet Isaiah calls out loud and clear to all that can hear. Charles Spurgeon once wrote,

> Ho!—this is the gospel note; a short, significant appeal, urging you to be wise enough to attend to your own interests. Oh, the condescension of God! That he should, as it were, become a beggar to his own creature, and stoop from the magnificence of his glory to cry, "Ho!" to foolish and ungrateful men! ("Enduring Word" Bible commentary by David Guzik)

Commentary writer David Guzik calls Isaiah 55 an invitation to receive the glory of the Lord's restoration. Hallelujah! He writes:

> Everyone who thirsts, come to the waters: It is an invitation to everyone—but everyone who thirsts. Only those who thirst will come to the waters. If we aren't thirsty for what the Lord can give us, then we will never come to His waters. ("Enduring Word" by David Guzik)

That's another link to the statement that our greatest need becomes our greatest opportunity to experience the love and power of God. Those in need, those who thirst, will come to the Living Water. Our greatest need, our greatest hurt, is an invitation to more of Jesus. Do you believe that? Have you already experienced this in your life? If so, how?

_____

_____

Who is this God who would bend down from heaven to reach you? To invite you in to His family. To call out your name. To love you right where you are. Do you struggle to believe the blood of Jesus is sufficient to remove the stain of your sin? Do you take the cross for granted? Write about the cross and what you believe about it. Write with your heart. Jesus knows it all.

Romans 5:8 tells us, "God demonstrated His own love for us in this: while we were still sinners, Christ died for us." Romans 4:25 says, "He was delivered over to death for our sins and was raised to life for our justification." God sent His Son to die for our sins. Every sin. Every person who believes in Jesus is saved by grace through faith. It is finished. In what ways have you struggled with shame from your past? What have you struggled to nail to the cross?

"WHO DO YOU SAY I AM?"

Write out a prayer of surrender for that thing you have held back from Jesus. Remember to include thanksgiving for what He did for you on the cross and what He is doing for you now.

Dig Deeper
Who do you say I am?

Read Matthew 16:13–18. The most important part of being a Christian is to know Jesus and know His nature. This first discipleship question, asked by Jesus himself, invites us to get a better understanding of who He is. *What we know and believe about Jesus determines how we live.*

This passage of Scripture is a critical conversation. Here we see Peter's recognition of Jesus's true identity. Jesus responds that on that truth He will build His Church and the gates of hell won't prevail against it! It is not only important for us to recognize the deity of Jesus, but also that our own identity is eternally linked to

Him. What we believe determines how we live. When we know who He is, then we know who we are. It's through knowing our Father that we can fully know and love ourselves.

Knowing God is vital to knowing oneself.

When we know who He is, then we understand our identity as heirs to all He has and all He is. Genesis 1:27 tells us we are made in God's image—our identity is in Him. "So God created human beings in his own image. In the image of God he created them; male and female he created them" (Genesis 1:27).

At the recognition of who Jesus is, Peter and the others knew who they were as sons of God and went out to build the Church. They knew who they were, therefore they knew what to do as His disciples. We are all sent to build the Church!

I encourage you to sit at your kitchen table with a cup of coffee early one morning and imagine Jesus is sitting across from you talking with you. He actually is there with you. Consider writing a list of His attributes. How would you describe Him from A to Z? For example, Abba, Best Friend, Comforter, Defender, etc.

_____
_____
_____
_____
_____
_____
_____
_____
_____

My goal is that by the end of this study, you will have more confidence and clarity in who Jesus is. Jesus often reveals Himself in our lives in different ways according to what He wants to teach and grow in us. If you're struggling with loneliness, Jesus may show Himself to you as your Best Friend. If you're working through father issues, He may show Himself to you as a loving and trustworthy Father.

"WHO DO YOU SAY I AM?"

Prayer Prompt

If you're not already meeting with Jesus daily, this week work on setting at least ten minutes aside to meet with Him. I recommend the morning, if possible, before everyone gets up in your house. I've been meeting with Jesus every morning for the past ten years. At first it was difficult, but I prayed the Holy Spirit would help me get out of bed, and He did! After a couple of weeks, I loved getting up early. Start with ten minutes and you will be amazed at the hunger for more of Jesus that grows within you.

In this prayer time, focus on telling Jesus who He is to you. If you are alone, speak it out loud. Talk to Him as if He's there with you—because He is. This is a time to get to know His character on a deeper, more intimate level. He delights in you and invites you to delight in Hm.

Jesus, you are my _____

_____
_____
_____
_____
_____
_____
_____
_____
_____

WEEK 3

"Do You Understand What I've Done for You?"

John 13:12

IN 2000, I WAS TWENTY-NINE YEARS OLD AND FELT LIKE I'D already lived several lives. That year, I met the man I would marry. Marriage, children, career. I'd grown up. I was deeply blessed. But in many ways, I still lived in the past. A confirmed perfectionist, I wore my mask well and pretended to move on with my life. Worldly success came easy. But many nights my husband would find me late in the evening, lying on the bed tucked into the fetal position, crying. He would ask me what was wrong, and I wouldn't know what to say. I felt ashamed of who I was and believed that if people knew the real me, they could never love me. Depression had been an unwanted traveling companion for years, and sometimes it climbed into the driver's seat.

Jesus pursues us even in our times of greatest unworthiness. Bulimia was my secret drug of choice for many years. It became more than a way to stay perfect; it became a way to control my circumstances. Bulimia became a way to purge my pain. And even as a wife and mom, it was the crutch I would go to when dealing with the self-inflicted pain of perfectionism—always performing for love. But the Lord doesn't see things the way you see them.

People judge by outward appearance, but the Lord looks at the heart. (1 Samuel 16:7)

Right in the center of my storm, at the age of thirty-nine, I finally gave my life to Jesus. That's a powerful story and one I will write another day, but let me say it was like I had been wandering in the dark all my life, in fear of the light. Then the Light came, and fear fled. Light filled my heart, vision, and mind. Light penetrated the darkness of my soul. From the moment I experienced, believed, and received the total forgiveness and love of Jesus, I gave myself fully to Him, and I haven't stopped. "In him was life, and that life was the light of all mankind. The light shines in the darkness, and the darkness has not overcome it" (John 1:4–5).

Do you understand what Jesus has done in you, through you and for you?

We don't find Jesus. He has never been lost. He pursues us by His Spirit. It's His Spirit that woos us and draws us to Himself and *then* we finally surrender. Once we accept Jesus as our Savior, the Holy Spirit begins the regeneration process of helping us live out our new life in Christ. The Holy Spirit lives in us, empowering us with divine strength to do His will in the earth. It truly is a mighty and mysterious miracle, but God guaranteed He would seal us with the gift of His Holy Spirit to help us become more and more like Jesus as we seek to love and obey Him.

Let's take a look at God's banquet. Read Isaiah 55:1–2.

Who is invited? Take a minute to write your answer.

_____
_____
_____
_____
_____

"DO YOU UNDERSTAND WHAT I'VE DONE FOR YOU?"

_____
_____
_____

I've broken Isaiah 55:1–2 down into two simple categories: the poor (needy), and the rich (self-sufficient). The poor in verse 1 is indicated by, "even if you have no money!" The rich in verse 2 is indicated by, "why use your money on that which does not satisfy?" Which category do you see yourself in and why?

_____
_____
_____
_____
_____
_____
_____

In order to help you understand how poor and rich relates to you, I've chosen the adjectives "needy" and "self-sufficient."

What does it mean to be poor and needy? What does Jesus say to those who fall into this category?

_____
_____
_____
_____
_____
_____
_____

Jesus invites us to come as we are. He invites us to come without resources, time, or talent. To come in our lack of education, opportunity, influence, motivation, hope, and strength. Come in our shame, embarrassment, and humiliation. Come in our emotional, physical, and spiritual bankruptcy. We can come in our poverty and brokenness. Come! It's ridiculously and extravagantly free. Nothing is withheld. Take a few minutes to write about your neediness. Can you identify with one of the examples above?

_____
_____
_____
_____
_____
_____
_____
_____
_____
_____

Matthew 5:5 tells us, "Blessed are the poor in spirit, for theirs is the kingdom of heaven."

Let's look closer at self-sufficiency. When we rely on self to meet each need, we prevent ourselves from having an intimate relationship with Jesus because we're rooted in pride. He made us to need Him. He wants us to lean on Him, to cast our cares on Him. Second Corinthians 12:9 tells us His strength is made perfect in our weakness. When we are self-sufficient, we have no need of God. What does Jesus say to those who fall into this category?

Take a few minutes to write about areas in your life where you are finding identity in your self-sufficiency. Can you identify with any of these?

Your talent	Your money	Your career
Your strength	Your resources	Your power
Your influence	Your education/training	Your house
Your cars	Your family	Your comfort
Your accomplishments	Your title/status	

"DO YOU UNDERSTAND WHAT I'VE DONE FOR YOU?"

You have plenty, but you're burned out. You're tired of chasing, performing, and striving; tired of comparing, climbing, and competing for significance. Tired of searching for something to fill the growing void. You're tired of repeating the same cycles. We hunger and thirst, but we feed on that which never fills us. What void are you trying to fill?

Come to me all you who are weary and burdened, and I will give you rest. Take my yoke upon you and learn from me, for I am gentle and humble in heart, and you will find rest for your souls. For my yoke is easy and my burden is light. (Matthew 11:28–30)

Dig Deeper
Do you understand what I've done for you?

The disciples were able watch Jesus in action, and we can watch Jesus in action today too. He is alive and working in the world. In order to see Jesus in the world today, we must hunt for the good in people and circumstances. When we find the good, there is Jesus in us, through us, and for us. James 1:17 tells us, "Every good and perfect gift is from above, coming down from the Father of the heavenly lights, who does not change like shifting shadows." We hunt for the good to thank God, to magnify His character on earth. When we share with others what Jesus is doing in our lives, we live out what Paul wrote in Romans 1:12, that is, that you and I may be mutually encouraged by each other's faith. Not only are we encouraged by one another's faith, but by the praise reports of how Jesus is working in each other's lives. We act as eyewitnesses to the goodness of God.

Do you understand what I've done for you? Read John 13:1–17. Jesus is asking you this question just like when He asked the disciples if they understood what He had done for them when He washed their feet. Take a few minutes to pray and write in the space below. If you don't understand what He's doing in you, through you, or for you, that is okay too. Write that down. Writing it will help set your mind and heart in the position to receive answers.

_____
_____
_____
_____
_____
_____
_____
_____
_____
_____
_____

Prayer Prompt

I'm praying you can set time aside daily to meet with Jesus. This week sit with Jesus and tell Him what you think He's doing in you, through you, and for you. Through this study, the Holy Spirit is leading you to identify your greatest need. He helps you understand in your heart—not just your mind—that Jesus died on the cross for you and that He's still working on your behalf today. He nailed your shame to the cross. You are invited to His banquet of abundance. Give Him thanks. I encourage you to share with a sister in Christ, or in your study group.

Jesus, you are doing _____

WEEK 4

"Are You Listening to Me?"

Matthew 17:5

A FEW MONTHS AFTER SURRENDERING MY LIFE TO JESUS, I met a wonderful Christian couple at a home-based business meeting I hadn't even planned to attend. We spent the better part of our meeting sharing with each other about the goodness of Jesus in our lives. When we finally got down to talking about the business, they told me they recently retired from the mortgage industry. When I asked where they had worked, it turned out to be the same company where Kyle worked. The same company that had the fateful Christmas party fifteen years before. The same party that resulted in the death of my sister.

My thoughts raced. Had they been there that night? I asked them if they knew Kyle. My heart pounded as I said his name. They hesitated and looked at each other with uncertainty. Finally, she exclaimed, "Oh yes, there was an accident." I told them that was my sister. We all stood in stunned amazement. They told me they started working for that company only a few months after the accident, and that Don, the owner of the company—the man responsible for giving the keys to the drunk driver—the man I had been angry at for so many years—had become their best friend.

The next moment was like an out-of-body experience for me, like all the air had been sucked out of the room.

"Can I have Don's number?" I asked. They looked confused, and I quickly said, "I want to forgive him."

As soon as the words came from my lips, I panicked. *Wait, what? I don't want to forgive! How can I possibly do that?* But the Holy Spirit had prompted my heart.

> Bear with each other and forgive one another if any of you has a grievance against someone. Forgive as the Lord forgave you. (Colossians 3:13)

I stared at the phone number scrawled on the yellow sticky and trembled inside with fear. What would I say? What would *he* say? For years I had blamed him. Every year he and his wife hosted company Christmas parties at their home. They had a rule: if their employees were going to drink, they had to turn in their keys and stay at their home. During the night, Kyle approached Don and said he wanted to leave. There was a brief discussion about Kyle's level of intoxication, but Don gave his keys to him anyway. Witnesses later testified he was too drunk to drive. That night he killed my sister; her best friend, Cathy; and himself. My sister's boyfriend and Cathy's sister survived and daily endure the physical pain of that fatal night.

For several days I struggled with fear of making that phone call. My husband and I went to our pastors for guidance and prayer. They encouraged me to see this as an invitation to let forgiveness break the chains of the enemy, to set the captives free. Not just my chains, but Don's chains too. This was a calling from God to heal the sins of the past, to bring God's kingdom on earth as it is in heaven.

"Above all else, guard your heart, for everything you do flows from it" (Proverbs 4:23).

To get a better understanding of our hunger and thirst, we need to take a closer look at our heart. The heart is mentioned almost one thousand times in Scripture. The biblical heart is unlike our physical heart, yet they have something in common. The health

"ARE YOU LISTENING TO ME?"

of our physical and spiritual hearts has a dramatic impact on our quality of life.

The biblical heart consists of our thoughts (what I think), feelings (what I feel), desires (what I want), will (what I choose), and motives (why I do it). How we think and feel, what we want, what we choose, and why we choose it comes from our heart. It's no wonder God says to guard our hearts above all else! The condition of our heart impacts every area of our lives.

How does this knowledge affect your understanding of your emotional and spiritual health?

_____
_____
_____
_____
_____
_____
_____
_____
_____

Some of the most empowering steps we can take is to first become aware of our thoughts, and then to be in control of our thoughts. But where do our thoughts come from? They come from our beliefs, which are largely formed in early childhood. Our beliefs are shaped by the meaning we attach to our experiences. For example, if you were teased as a child for wearing glasses, you may believe that glasses make you unworthy of acceptance. Therefore, when you wear your glasses you feel insecure because you think about being unworthy. Our beliefs drive our thoughts. Our thoughts lead to emotions, our emotions lead to actions, and actions lead to results. Our results reinforce our beliefs. It's important that we reflect on our beliefs about God, ourselves and the world around us. It would be helpful to make note of some of your thoughts and trace them back to beliefs you may have. Are your beliefs true, or are they a deception? Do they line up with the truth of God's Word? Second Corinthians 10:5 says to take every thought captive to Christ. Our thoughts unchecked can lead to very destructive outcomes. But when we examine our thoughts and align them to the truth of God's Word, we can live a renewed and transformed life.

Have you ever thought about what you think about? Have you ever thought about what Jesus thinks about what you think about?

Now we are going to do a heart assessment. Let's invite the Holy Spirit to examine our hearts. There is no wholeness apart from God. Don't be afraid. For some of you, this may be the first time you have invited the Holy Spirit into the thorny places in your heart. There will be no condemnation, only gentle conviction, loving encouragement, and fresh revelation. Any condemnation you feel is from the enemy. We can recognize condemnation as a general feeling of failure. We recognize conviction as a direction from the Holy Spirit to correct something specific. Conviction brings repentance and restoration, while condemnation brings shame and guilt. The devil's mission is for you to stay wounded and stuck. Pray against his lies and meditate on God's love for you. This is your time. The Lord has invited you to this study for such a time as this to be freed. "Therefore, there is now no condemnation for those who are in Christ Jesus" (Romans 8:1).

Several years ago, I led a Celebrate Recovery ministry in a church we used to attend. One of the key tools I learned from recovery is the "HALT test," which stands for: Hungry, Angry, Lonely, and Tired. This tool helps people identify when they may be vulnerable to relapse. But the Lord has shown me a deeper meaning to HALT. This doesn't speak only to our physical needs, but to our spiritual and emotional needs as well.

Hungry
What do you do when you're hungry?

"ARE YOU LISTENING TO ME?"

Food is fuel, but what about when we use food to meet an unmet emotional need? We overindulge, abstain, or restrict. Food can become our enemy or our best friend, our comfort. It can be used to control our circumstances or to attain perfection. Any time we use food to meet a need, we "buy that which does not truly satisfy." What is your unmet need? Are you hungry for love, approval, acceptance, intimacy, recognition, influence, power, companionship? Something else? Sisters, we are made to crave. Made to hunger and thirst for righteousness. When we follow Jesus and turn to Him in our ravenous appetite, He will fill us. Hunger is soil for the seed of revival!

Take a few minutes to ask the Holy Spirit to show you what you're hungry for and to reveal what you go to in your hunger.

_____
_____
_____
_____
_____
_____
_____
_____
_____

> Then Jesus declared, 'I am the bread of life. Whoever comes to me will never go hungry, and whoever believes in me will never be thirsty.' (John 6:35)

Angry

What do you do when you're angry?

Anger is an indication something needs to be resolved. It's like a check engine light. When we fail to deal with anger, it hardens our heart and makes us bitter. For some, it leads to aggression, passive aggressiveness, revenge, or even violence. When we stuff our feelings of anger, it leads to resentment. We can stifle or repress anger, but eventually it overflows into other areas of our lives. Problems remain unresolved and we take it out on our relationships or learn to sustain them with emotional distance. Our relationships suffer. We suffer. Our relationship with God suffers. The kingdom suffers.

Do you gossip or slander others? Do you compete? Do you feel happy when someone doesn't do well? Those could be signs that you are harboring anger. Many experts agree that the root of anger is fear, which can come from rejection, abandonment, abuse, or other hurts. Take a few minutes to ask the Holy Spirit to show you the source of your anger and what you go to in your anger.

___
___
___
___
___
___
___
___
___
___

> In your anger do not sin: Do not let the sun go down while you are still angry, and do not give the devil a foothold. (Ephesians 4:26–27)

Lonely

What do you do when you're lonely?

Loneliness is the craving of intimacy. Humans are made with the desire for intimacy because we were created to be intimate with God. When craving is left unsatisfied, it can lead to isolation, attention-seeking behavior, and depression. Do you feel lonely in your marriage? Lonely in leadership? Lonely in your family or community of friends? Do you feel neglected, misunderstood, or left out? Take a few minutes and ask the Holy Spirit to reveal where you are lonely and what you go to in your loneliness.

___

Though my father and mother forsake me, the Lord will receive me. (Psalm 27:10)

Tired

What do you do when you're tired?

Today's culture moves at lightning speed. We often say yes to too many things, as if a packed calendar is a sign of significance. We are overscheduled, overtired, and overstimulated. Our minds and bodies need rest. Striving to get ahead is an indication that we don't trust God to provide. Hustle is glamorized, while the power of rest is underestimated. Social media is partly to blame, as it intensifies the feeling of comparison and the need to keep up with everyone else, leading to burnout and depression.

In your tiredness, do you become negative and irritable? Do you lack the ability to resist temptation when you're tired? Do you become impatient and lose perspective? Are you tired of a situation or an unanswered prayer? Tired of performing, pushing, striving? Tired of serving?

Take a few minutes and ask the Holy Spirit to show you where you are tired and what you go to in your exhaustion.

_____
_____
_____
_____
_____
_____
_____
_____
_____

> Come to me, all you who are weary and burdened, and I will give you rest. Take my yoke upon you and learn from me, for I am gentle and humble in heart, and you will find rest for your souls. For my yoke is easy and my burden is light. (Matthew 11:28–30)

If our heart is vulnerable in any of these areas, we must "HALT" and reconnect to the Bread of Life, the Living Water, or we will slip back into our self-made hiding places. We will stumble into captivity to our pain. We must guard our hearts not only from the effects of our wounds but also from the lies of the enemy. "Stay alert! Watch out for your great enemy, the devil. He prowls around like a roaring lion, looking for someone to devour" (1 Peter 5:8).

One reason we don't "HALT" and reconnect is because we are too busy and distracted. Busyness is often the biggest block to the voice of God. We must reprioritize and make Him first in our lives. Many of us strive for balance in all our busyness. There are countless magazine articles, podcasts, and books about finding balance in the modern life. But life is less about balance and more about alignment. Aligning our lives with the will of God. This is where you will find peace and power. Alignment is centering ourselves with His presence and recognizing who He is and who we are in Him. It's allowing our heart to receive His love. It's aligning ourselves in intimacy with Jesus and operating out of that sacred place.

Think about when the tires on your car are out of alignment. The whole car wobbles down the road, jarring everything inside of it. When your tires are aligned, everything is in balance. Align yourself with heaven to gain life balance. "The thief comes only to steal and kill and destroy; I have come that they may have life, and have it to the full" (John 10:10).

What has the Lord shown you through this heart assessment? What have you learned? Write about it.

_____
_____
_____
_____
_____
_____
_____
_____
_____
_____

Dig Deeper

Are you listening to Me?

In this generation, I see many people chasing encounters with God. Although we can absolutely encounter God, we must be rooted in God's Word. We are called to be people of His Word, to pursue and obey it. His Word is power. It is alive. It is sharper than any two-edged sword. It is personal. His Word is a love letter to you and me. This question teaches us how to listen to the Lord through His Word. A powerful practice while reading Scripture is to personalize it. Put your name in it. This will help you listen to Him.

Read Matthew 17:1–5. Peter, James, and John witness the transfiguration of Jesus as He meets with Moses and Elijah. God speaks from heaven and says, "This is my Son whom I dearly love and whom gives me great joy. Listen to him" (Matthew 17:5). The transfiguration reveals the deity of Christ. It reveals the identity and glory of Christ. God commands us to listen to His Son, with whom He is well pleased. Have you given Jesus this authority in your life?

Isaiah 55:3–4 says, "Come to me with your ears wide open. Listen, and you will find life." What is Jesus speaking to you through this study right now? What is he saying to you through his Word? Write about it.

_____
_____
_____
_____
_____
_____
_____
_____
_____
_____
_____
_____

Prayer Prompt

You have done well, sister! I'm so proud of the heart work you are doing and how you are prioritizing daily meeting with Jesus. This week I want you to pray about the areas in your heart the Holy Spirit identified as being vulnerable to lies. Do you have areas of unforgiveness in your heart? Who do you need to forgive? Yourself? Others? God?

Will you do it? Remember who He is to you and what He is doing in you as you pray through this lesson.

_____
_____
_____
_____
_____
_____
_____

WEEK 5

"Do You Really Love Me?"

John 21:15–19

A WEEK AFTER I GOT DON'S PHONE NUMBER, I CALLED HIM. IT was a conversation I will never forget and one I share about often. I mostly listened as he went through a myriad of emotions on the other end of the line: shock, anger, remorse, indignation, surrender. He asked me how I had the courage to call him. No one from the families of the victims ever had reached out to him. I told him it was Jesus. Jesus had forgiven me so much, how could I not extend the same forgiveness?

I had never thought about what he and his family lost that night. I never thought about what he might have had to live through—the guilt and regret. I only thought of myself because pain makes us selfish. Think about when you stub your toe really hard or cut your finger. All you can think about is the pain; nothing else going on around you matters. Emotional pain is the same way. You become intensely self-focused. I told him I had made poor decisions in my life, but I was lucky none of them ever took a life. I was given grace when I didn't deserve it. He made a bad decision, and there is grace and mercy for him too.

I hung up the phone and sat in awe. In that moment, I felt a thousand pounds lift from my shoulders. Weight I didn't even realize I carried, a burden that had become a part of me.

In that moment, I was also able to forgive my father for the pain he caused my mom, my sister, and me. I finally saw him as a broken man who loved me with the capacity he could. I was able to forgive God. I had carried anger because He didn't prevent my sister's accident. I realized that although He didn't prevent it, He was the only one who could redeem it. And I was able to forgive myself. I had learned to be so hard on myself. For most of my life I carried responsibility that was not mine to carry—responsibility groomed by codependency from my childhood.

> And all the trees of the field shall clap their hands. Instead of the thorn shall come up the cypress tree, And instead of the brier shall come up the myrtle tree. (Isaiah 55:12–13)

When we harbor hurts (letting them fester into bitterness and resentment), they hold us captive. A bitter root forms in our heart that gives life to the growth of thorns. What does the Lord say about a bitter root?

> In every relationship, be swift to choose peace over power; run toward holiness, for those who are not holy will not see the Lord. Watch over each other to make sure that no one misses the revelation of God's grace. And make sure no one lives with a root of bitterness sprouting within them which will only cause trouble and poison the hearts of many. (Hebrews 12:14–15 TPT)

Bitterness grows deep within the soil of our hearts, barely noticeable until it produces a harvest of pain in our lives and in those we love and care about. It affects how we see and treat people. We often think we can modify the behaviors a bitter root causes. But the freedom Christ promises does not come from a behavior modification program. It's true freedom that comes from letting Him help you pull the root out!

The prophet Isaiah in verse 55:13 says to those who eat of the Lord's banquet of abundance, thorns will be replaced by the cypress tree and briers replaced by the myrtle tree. The thorn is prickly, hard, and rigid and exists to protect the plant. The brier is a thicket of thorns. Imagine a thicket of thorns growing in and around your heart, ensuring that nothing gets in and nothing gets out.

The cypress tree is an evergreen, holding on to its dense leaves in and out of season. The myrtle is a very special tree indeed. It produces fragrant blossoms and edible fruit. It symbolizes the recovery and establishment of God's promises.

I love this picture of transformation. This is the fruit of life in Christ, of feasting at God's banquet of abundance. How does knowledge about the five parts of your spiritual heart (your thoughts, feelings, desires, will, and motives) help you understand the effects of thorns that might grow in your heart?

_____
_____
_____
_____
_____
_____
_____
_____
_____
_____
_____

Maybe you are already experiencing life like the myrtle tree. What do you think that means about the condition of your heart?

_____
_____
_____
_____
_____
_____
_____
_____
_____
_____

In order to have freedom from the bitter root that causes emotional and relational bondage, we must pull it out. Here's how we can remove the root in four steps:

1. Pray. We can't do this on our own. We need God's grace and mercy. Throughout this study the Holy Spirit has been leading you to assess your heart as He has helped you identify your greatest need. But He's not finished. He reveals what He will heal. Pray for His strength and power to help you take the next steps to freedom. Pray for His wisdom and discernment to know what the next steps are for you. Pray for healing. But prayer isn't only about what God can do for you, but about spending time with Him. Prayer is the language of intimate relationship with Jesus. Write out your prayer.

_____
_____
_____
_____
_____
_____
_____

"DO YOU REALLY LOVE ME?"

2. Obey. This is the part we often put off, mostly out of pride or fear. Our pride comes from the lie of self-sufficiency. We convince ourselves we can do it on our own, or that we are enough in our own achievements. The devil doesn't mind helping us hold on to this wrong belief. Our fear comes from many places, but the fear of change comes from a fear of the unknown. Sometimes we've believed lies about ourselves for so long that we don't know who we'd be without them. We are afraid of failure. We're afraid of success. Sometimes our fear is from spiritual attack. Are you struggling to obey something He has asked you to do? Are there amends you need to make? Ask the Holy Spirit to reveal to you what blocks your obedience. Is it pride or fear? Or is it something else? Write about it.

3. Forgive. One of the greatest tools of torment is unforgiveness, which makes forgiveness one of the most powerful weapons of warfare against our enemy and against the bitter root systems in our heart. Unforgiveness is like drinking poison and expecting the other person to die. Forgiveness is not a feeling, it's a choice, and one that may need to be made repeatedly as the Holy Spirit helps your heart and feelings catch up. There is no restoration without forgiveness. God's Word has plenty to

say about forgiveness. Read Matthew 18:21-35. What do these verses tell us about Jesus?

_____

What does verse 34 mean? Could there be a spiritual curse that comes with unforgiveness?

_____

I stated earlier that the greatest tool of torment is unforgiveness. Who is the Holy Spirit bringing to your mind that you need to forgive? Is it yourself? Others? God? Say the name or names out loud and then write them down here. "I forgive _____."

_____

"DO YOU REALLY LOVE ME?"

4. Replace. When you engage in the process of heart healing you begin to clear it out and must be careful to fill the space with the truth of God. Think of your heart like a garden. You till the soil and plant seeds of beautiful vegetables and flowers, but thorny weeds easily grow in the fresh soil. You must be diligent to pull those weeds before they overrun the garden. Where in your life can you pull out weeds of unforgiveness, bitterness, and resentment? You must replace the lies with truth.

Read Luke 11:24–26. What lies are you believing about yourself? Identify a lie you believe and then find a truth in Scripture to replace it with. For example, if you believe the lie that you can't break free from your past, look to verses like 2 Corinthians 5:17. Read it out loud every time you need a reminder that you are not defined by your past. Better yet, write it in your journal and make it a daily affirmation. Repeat this process with other lies you are believing. This is what taking each thought captive means.

Repeat these steps as many times as you need throughout your life. Persevere in this and make it a way of life; asking for forgiveness, forgiving others, planting yourself in the truth of God's Word, and doing what He says.

What does it mean to eat at the Lord's banquet of abundance?

When we turn to the Lord, listen to Him, and do what He says, we feast at His banquet of abundance and experience His promise of restoration. Unfortunately, we often feast at the wrong table: the table set by culture, our pain, or our enemy. Feasting at His banquet means having an intimate relationship with God where we seek Him and enjoy His company. It means spending time with Him and delighting in His presence. That is why I've included the five discipleship questions so you will have a plan to help develop your intimacy with Jesus.

Dig Deeper
Do you really love Me?

Our love for Jesus should manifest in our love and service to people. We can't earn our salvation, but faith without works is dead. In John 21:15–18, Jesus asks Peter three times if he loves Him. Each time Peter responds with increasing urgency and concern that Jesus doubts his love. But Jesus is actually emphasizing what loving Him really looks like. Feeding His sheep. Serving and caring for His people. This question helps us to evaluate our level of love for Jesus. The "sheep" that Jesus is referring to can be broken down into four categories:

1. You: Sometimes you are the sheep that needs feeding. Reflect on your HALT assessment. Do you need to prioritize yourself to be fed and cared for by Jesus? Do you need to take better care of yourself spiritually, emotionally, or physically? We should start with ourselves. We can't feed people from an

empty basket. Is the Lord prompting you to make time for Him to care for you? Will you do it?

2. Your family: Is the Lord calling you to feed and care for someone in your family? Husband, children, in-laws? Will you do it?

3. The church: Is the Lord putting someone specifically on your heart in the church to care for? Who is He nudging you to disciple? Will you do it?

4. The lost: Jesus came to seek and to save the lost. What lost person is Jesus asking you to feed and care for? Will you do it?

When believers tell me they don't have a heart for the lost, my first question is, "How's your intimacy?" Jesus has a heart for the lost. If we don't, we have to ask ourselves if we are really connected to the heart of God.

What are you sensing from the Holy Spirit about these four types of sheep?

_____
_____
_____
_____
_____
_____
_____
_____
_____
_____

Prayer Prompt
This has been another intense week. I pray you are encouraged and strengthened in this work by the Holy Spirit. Pray this week for the Lord to set your heart ablaze with a fire for more of Him. Pray for deeper trust of His goodness and faithfulness. Pray He will help you let go of anything you are holding on to that doesn't serve you

or your relationships. I pray you are now getting into a rhythm and routine of spending quality time with Jesus. Remember, when you read the Word, personalize it. Put your name into the Scriptures and let the Lord speak to you personally.

You may connect with other women in the study, and that's wonderful! Remember, you are not alone.

_____
_____
_____
_____
_____
_____
_____
_____
_____
_____
_____

WEEK 6

"Do You Believe Me?"

John 11:25-26

A COUPLE MONTHS AFTER MY ENCOUNTER WITH THE POWER of forgiveness, I sat in my room, praising Jesus for His faithfulness as I read my journal entries. I thought about how I'd been captivated by an intense love, joy, and peace I'd never known. A freedom I didn't think possible. As I reflected, I sat upright and realized I hadn't been counting calories or been consumed with worry about what I would eat, or how I would get rid of it. In fact, I hadn't purged in months! I had a good span of time in the past where I didn't indulge in my eating disorder, but I'd always obsessed about food and its consequences. But now it was gone! No thought. No worry. No obsession!

Twelve years later and I have not had one thought or one incident of my bulimia. I'm completely free and healed of the eating disorder that imprisoned me for almost twenty years. The power of forgiveness is unstoppable, unshakable, and unsurpassable! We are completely forgiven in Christ when we accept his gift of forgiveness and trust Him with our past, present, and future. When we trust Him with our hearts and allow Him to be the Lord of our lives, we forsake our own way so that we may walk in His will. Then, we become a new human being. As followers of Jesus, we are a new human walking this earth with kingdom influence and power.

Forgiven and free forever.

Our battle is not against flesh and blood, but against an actual enemy in the spiritual realm. The devil's strategy is to deceive us, lock us up in resentment, bitterness, and confusion. To render us useless. But forgiveness is a weapon of heaven's army, forged by the King of Kings himself to set the captives free. Will you pick up your weapon today?

Humans long for purpose. A purpose that fulfills the reason we exist. God's Word tells us we are His masterpiece and He created us in Christ to "do good works that he has prepared in advance for us to do" (Ephesians 2:10). Some people are born knowing their purpose, like being a doctor, a teacher, or a pastor, while others struggle along, doubting they will ever know. I believe much of the hopelessness, depression, and addiction in our world is born in the depths of a soul yearning for purpose and meaning. I've heard it said that the two most important days in your life are the day you were born and the day you find out why. When you discover your purpose, you become fully awake.

We are all gifted and called to specific purposes, but our ultimate purpose is to love God and love people.

> Jesus replied, "'You must love the Lord your God with all your heart, all your soul, and all your mind.' This is the first and greatest commandment. A second is equally important: 'Love your neighbor as yourself.' The entire law and all the demands of the prophets are based on these two commandments." (Matthew 22:37–40 NLT)

Every day we are given the grace to do just that. We find our daily purpose loving others in the places God puts us.

Years ago, I sensed the Lord wanted me to connect with a Muslim neighbor. Even though we have different beliefs about who God is, we forged a wonderful friendship, and I had the blessing to walk with her through some hard things, such as cancer and divorce. It's been an honor and a blessing to come alongside her with the love of Jesus.

But there's a specific calling, vision, or mission God has written across our hearts. The Bible tells us people perish without vision. We are made in God's image, and He seeds us with vision to bring His dreams to life on earth.

In Isaiah 55, we hear the prophet prophesy about God's promise of purpose for those who hunger and thirst for Him. He fulfilled that promise in and through David, and extends the same promises to us.

> Give ear and come to me;
> listen, that you may live.
> I will make an everlasting covenant with you,
> my faithful love promised to David.
> See, I have made him a witness to the peoples,
> a ruler and commander of the peoples.
> Surely you will summon nations you know not,
> and nations you do not know will come running to you,
> because of the LORD your God,
> the Holy One of Israel,
> for he has endowed you with splendor. (Isaiah 55:3–5 NIV)

God called David to be king, but gifted him to act as a witness, leader, commander and evangelist. More importantly, these verses foreshadow who Christ would be for all of us. These four roles are not an exhaustive list of callings and purpose, but they are critical roles within the Kingdom of God today.

Witness

A witness is a person who testifies to an event or provides proof. In John 1, Jesus called John the Baptist a witness who testified concerning the light so through him all might believe. In Acts 1:8, it's promised we will receive power when the Holy Spirit comes on us, and we will be His witnesses in Jerusalem, Judea, Samaria, and to the ends of the earth. What does that mean to you in your areas of influence? What's holding you back from witnessing?

How has He equipped you for this purpose?

_____
_____
_____
_____
_____
_____
_____
_____
_____
_____

How has He positioned you for this purpose?

_____
_____
_____
_____
_____
_____
_____
_____
_____
_____

Leader

A leader is typically someone who motivates people along a certain vision or mission.

Martin Luther King Jr. gave the famous speech that started with "I have a dream" and sparked the vision, commitment, and inspiration of an entire generation. The Bible is clear that a leader is to lead by the example set by Jesus. A biblical leader should be a servant leader, one who serves with vision, humility, love, integrity, and lives out the Word of God. That type of leadership is one that compels people to walk through any circumstance and overcome any obstacle to follow that leader. That kind of leadership inspires people to go against the status quo to accomplish the vision. In our current post-Christian culture, this leadership is sorely lacking. We desperately need leaders who will lead this generation to its highest calling in an age of doubt, deception, and division.

Has He equipped you for this purpose?

_____
_____
_____
_____
_____
_____
_____
_____
_____

How has He positioned you for this purpose?

_____
_____
_____
_____
_____
_____
_____
_____
_____

Commander

The definitions of *commander* and *leader* are very similar, however, commander has a military connotation. It signifies military authority. We are all called to be soldiers in the army of God. We all have a mission. The Bible talks about the battle every believer must fight in the spiritual realm against the enemy, the world, and even himself. The vision of God raising up an army stirs our spiritual senses and rallies our courage. As our culture slips further from the ways of God, there is an uprising of culture changers—an army who believes God is who He says He is. God is calling up commanders to lead the charge who will lead with spiritual authority. They will lead an army who is willing and ready to fight with the Word of God, the sword of the Spirit, and the truth in love. We all have authority in Christ, but there are commanders being called who have the spiritual authority to give instruction and lead an army for the cause of Christ.

How has He equipped you for this purpose?

_____
_____
_____
_____
_____
_____
_____
_____
_____
_____

How has He positioned you for this purpose?

_____
_____
_____
_____
_____
_____
_____
_____
_____
_____

"DO YOU BELIEVE ME?"

Evangelist

An evangelist is someone who seeks to convert others to the Christian faith, especially through public preaching. However, it's not limited to public preaching. The Bible has plenty to say about evangelism. We are all called to evangelize and win others over for Jesus. The Bible tells us that evangelism is for every follower of Christ. Matthew 28:19–20 says, "Go and make disciples of all nations, baptizing them in the name of the Father, and of the Son and of the Holy Spirit, teaching them to obey everything I have commanded you. And surely I am with you always to the very end of the age."

Some people are called to be evangelists, but all of us are called to evangelize. One of the most effective ways is to share your story. People can argue about theology, but they can't argue about your experience. What does 1 Peter 3:15 say about evangelism?

Have you ever written out your testimony? How can you share your story? With whom?

_____
_____
_____
_____
_____
_____
_____

According to Revelation 12:11, our testimonies carry great power: "They triumphed over him by the blood of the Lamb and the word of their testimony." They overcame the accuser by the blood of Jesus and their bold stories of their witness. Consider how you could share your testimony of coming to Christ, or the things Jesus has helped you persevere through by faith.

If you are doing this study with a group, take five minutes and share your story with a woman in your group. Share who you were before Christ, how you came to Christ, and your life in Christ now.

How has He equipped you for this purpose?

_____
_____
_____
_____
_____
_____
_____
_____

How has He positioned you for this purpose?

_____
_____
_____
_____
_____
_____
_____
_____
_____

David was anointed leader and king for the people, not of the people. He was assigned, appointed, and anointed by God for a predetermined time in history, for a distinct purpose and calling.

You have been assigned, appointed, and anointed for this predetermined time in history—for a distinct purpose and calling. When you allow the Lord into your greatest need, you will experience His love and power, which will be the source of your greatest authority in Christ.

Our authority comes from Jesus. We walk in His authority because we believe in His work on the cross and because the Holy Spirit lives in us. We are heirs to the kingdom of God. But many believers walk in powerlessness, unaware of their authority in Christ.

There are a few reasons for this, but one is when we keep parts of our lives and hearts off limits to Jesus. When we keep distance between ourselves and Jesus, we are more prone to unbelief. Unbelief limits our view of our authority in Christ. When we allow Jesus full access to our lives and respond in obedience, we can't be stopped!

Doing heart work increases our capacity. There's more room for the Lord to work in and through us. When the Lord increases our capacity, He increases our authority. Jesus isn't expecting perfection. He's asking us to follow Him and let His grace and truth perfect us. We will stumble, but we must get back up with our hearts aimed for His.

Dig Deeper
Do you believe Me?

This question provides you an opportunity to affirm not only that you believe IN Jesus, but that you believe Jesus. Do you believe He can and will turn your pain into purpose for your good and His glory? Do you believe that He is able to redeem and restore you? Read Ephesians 2:10. You are made with a plan and purpose in mind and there is good work set aside for you to do.

Sometimes we get so distracted by our own problems that we forget we are to live on mission. We have the supernatural power of the Holy Spirit living inside of us! We are world changers and the world is in desperate need of us living like we believe Jesus!

Read John 11:25-26

Do you believe in Jesus, sister? Do you believe in Him for your salvation? Do you believe He is who He says He is? Write about it.

_____
_____
_____
_____
_____
_____

Prayer Prompt

I encourage you this week to pray for your purpose. Pray to believe you are fearfully and wonderfully made and you have *not* been disqualified for the vision and purpose God has for your life. Take a step of faith and watch His faithfulness.

As You Rise

SISTERS, WE HAVE JOURNEYED TOGETHER FOR SIX WEEKS, opening the deepest parts of our hearts to the healing hand of the Lord. The Holy Spirit has shown us our greatest need and taught us it's our greatest opportunity to experience His love and power. Because after all, our greatest need is actually for Jesus himself. We have invited Jesus to disciple us through the Holy Spirit's leading and guidance. We have identified the lies of the enemy and where they took root in our lives. We have listened and obeyed. We have given ourselves grace to be vulnerable as we've shared and encouraged one another. We have believed together that the Lord has a great purpose for our lives, and we are created for more. We know we are not disqualified, and He will use our mess for His message of redemption and restoration. We have glimpsed the glory of God and understood we are kingdom builders.

May we rise and rejoice as we take our places as daughters of the Most High King! We are a rising army, fighting our battles with the Word of God, wielding the sword of the Spirit, speaking truth in love, and putting all of our trust in King Jesus. We are the bride of Christ, and our Bridegroom is coming. Let's get ready!

We have tasted freedom together. And now we fight for freedom for those around us, no longer locked up in ourselves, but bringing heaven to earth.

Now, my beloved ones, I have saved these important truths to send you off:

Be supernaturally infused with strength through your union with the Lord Jesus.

Stand victorious with the force of his explosive power flowing in and through you. Put on God's complete set of armor provided for us, so that you will be protected as you fight against the evil strategies of the accuser. Your hand-to-hand combat is not with human beings, but with the highest principalities operating in rebellion under the heavenly realms. For they are a powerful class of demons and evil spirits that hold this dark world in bondage. Because of this, you must wear the armor God provides so you're protected as you confront the slanderer, for you are destined for all things and will rise victorious. (Ephesians 6:10–13 TPT)

My Prayer for You
Father God, thank you for this powerful time with You and my beautiful sisters! Thank you for Your Word that heals and restores and does not return void. Thank you for the hunger You have set in our hearts—the hunger for more of You. Thank you that in You we are fully satisfied. I pray that we no longer believe the lies of the enemy or the culture that tell us You are not enough. You are more than enough, and in You we are more than conquerors! I pray we continue to replace every lie with Your Word through the power of Your Holy Spirit. "May we forget what is behind and strain forward to what is ahead, pressing on toward the goal to win the prize for which you have called us heavenward in Christ Jesus" (Philippians 3:13). In Jesus's holy name, amen.

Acknowledgments

OVER THE YEARS I'VE HAD THE BLESSING OF BEING MENTORED by Hal and Debbi Perkins, a wonderful, Spirit-filled couple who developed a simple yet powerful discipleship model. This model is patterned from questions Jesus asked his own disciples and is designed to be used as a tool for making disciple makers.

Hal was a youth pastor and pastor for forty years. Before the call to ministry, he had been a math teacher and coach and felt terribly ill-equipped. Discipleship wasn't a big topic in church culture at that time.

The Lord led him on a journey of discovery into His heart for discipleship that eventually produced the model I have used in this study in the Dig Deeper sections. After forty years of ministry, the Perkinses sold their home and obeyed the call to travel the country making disciples who make disciples.

This discipleship model has impacted my life significantly by increasing my intimacy with Jesus and giving me a way to help others do the same. Hal has written several excellent books, including *If Jesus Were A Parent*, *Walk with Me*, and *Discipled by Jesus*.

When believers get together in small groups to grow their faith together, they spend a lot of time talking about Jesus. That's not wrong, but the purpose of this method is to help believers talk to Jesus, to listen for His responses, and do what he says.

In *Discipled by Jesus* groups there is a facilitator who follows the leading of the Holy Spirit to guide the group through the five discipleship questions I've included in the "Dig Deeper" sections at the end of each week.

The purpose of the group is for each person to be discipled by Jesus. The goal is that members of the group will grow as facilitators themselves and start their own discipleship groups. This model enables multiplication of disciple makers.

I have been practicing these five questions for years in my quiet time with the Lord, as well as leading groups with them, and making disciple makers. If you would like coaching on this discipleship model, please contact me at www.Riseandrejoiceministries.com or Hal and Debbi Perkins at https://discipledbyjesus.org/.

About the Author

Heather Murdock is a speaker and author called to prepare the bride of Christ; to fan the flame of love and devotion for Jesus. She has a passion to encourage and equip believers to live Spirit-empowered lives so they can overcome obstacles and live out their purpose. Her podcast, Fanning the Flame with Heather Murdock, is a great discipleship resource to help fan the flame of love and devotion to Jesus. She draws from numerous life experiences, her passion for intimacy with Jesus and the Word of God. Heather travels in her role as vice president of human resources for a global manufacturing tech company, developing leaders and company culture, but her favorite place is with her family. They live in Placerville, California, where they serve in their local church. She and her husband are cofounders of Rise and Rejoice Ministries, which focuses on kingdom discipleship, Spirit-filled worship, and outreach.

Facebook: www.facebook.com/heather.murdock.author/
Instagram: www.instagram.com/heather.murdock
TikTok: vm.tiktok.com/@heathermurdock1

Additional resources, including teaching videos for this study, can be found on Heather's website: www.riseandrejoiceministries.com

Order Information

To order additional copies of this book, please visit
www.redemption-press.com.
Also available at Christian bookstores and Barnes and Noble.

CPSIA information can be obtained
at www.ICGtesting.com
Printed in the USA
BVHW030315150323
660407BV00002B/571